MARIANNE DE TREY

RICHARD DENNIS
2007

ACKNOWLEDGEMENTS

This catalogue has been inspired by the retrospective exhibition of Marianne de Trey's work at the gallery of the Devon Guild of Craftsmen in Bovey Tracey, 2007.

The informative and perceptive essay on Marianne de Trey's life and work was written by David Whiting. It is a revised version of the essay written for the Bristol Guild which was published, together with David's chronology, in their catalogue of 2006. Marianne's memoirs were first published in the High Cross House Exhibition Catalogue of 1995. We are grateful for permission to reprint both David's essay and Marianne's memoirs.

All the pots illustrated in colour were in the 2007 exhibition. They were selected by Margot Coatts and the exhibition was curated by Dee Martin. The majority of the pots are from Marianne's collection, several pieces were lent by Andy Christian and Christine Halstead, acknowledged in this catalogue as *A.C. Coll* and *C.H. Coll*. Two of the colour images are courtesy of David Westwood.

Richard Dennis

Editing and production by Sue Evans
Colour photography by Magnus Dennis
Print and reproduction by Flaydemouse, Yeovil, Somerset
Published by Richard Dennis, The Old Chapel, Shepton Beauchamp, Somerset TA19 OLE
©2007 Richard Dennis, David Whiting and Marianne de Trey
ISBN 978-0-903685-00-9
British Library Cataloguing-in-Publication Data.
A catalogue record for this book is available from the British Library

MARIANNE DE TREY – A BIOGRAPHY

Marianne de Trey CBE is now, unbelievably, in her seventh decade of making. This eternally youthful and very independent potter may have slowed down just a *little* in recent years, but she still has the prodigious energy of someone much younger, of someone with a mission, an undimmed sense of enquiry. In Marianne's company one is always able to discuss the widest range of topics – from the newest development on the ceramic scene, in which she continues to take an active interest, to the political situation in the modern world. She has long-held liberal and egalitarian values which have guided the principles of her life and work. It is in this context that her pots are best appreciated, as part of her commitment to an improved and healthier society, in which the crafts play their role, as part of a more balanced economy, and as an enrichment to the lives of ordinary people. And Marianne has unusually strong ties with the creative life of Dartington in Devon, where she is now something of a legend, coming as she did to this place just after the last war with her late husband, the potter Sam Haile. 'The Cabin', the functional wooden house in which she has always lived at Shinners Bridge, is now almost as familiar a part of the local landscape as Dartington Hall, the centre of the arts community Marianne has helped to lead for over half a century.

Those who know Marianne will attest to her modesty of character, and a certain austerity of lifestyle. In common with many potters of her generation, she has little interest in material things and has her own – largely seasonal – rhythm of working. But her upbringing, by contrast, was quite privileged and conventional. She was born in 1913 to upper-middle class Swiss parents. Her businessman father had, however, aspired to be an architect and was sympathetic to Marianne's restless and creative hands – he knew about materials and tools and 'right-doing'. De Trey's art teacher at her strict-sounding boarding school advised Marianne to go to the Royal College of Art in South Kensington. Here, after some exploration, she became drawn to textiles, in which she was awarded a diploma in 1936, going on to teach the subject briefly at Ipswich School of Art. It was at the RCA that she met fellow student, Sam Haile, an attractive and charismatic figure who would go on to become one of Britain's leading young potters and painters. London-born Haile, who was to join the English Surrealist Group in 1937, came from a very different background to de Trey. Of working class origins, he had contempt for the conservative attitudes which had shaped Marianne's upbringing and was able to introduce her to a much broader world, not only of the visual arts but of literature, music and politics. Certainly Marianne's democratic conscience owes much to Haile's radical outlook.

They married in 1938 and subsequently moved to the USA where Sam exhibited the boldly expressive brush and slip decorated pots recently made in England. The impact made by this work led to a teaching post for Haile at Alfred University, a major centre for American ceramics and where, after a period of designing textiles, Marianne herself began to learn about the rudiments of pottery, using the college facilities for the purpose. The sale of Haile's innovative work quickly established his name in America, but Marianne made her own mark. When, after a period at the University of Michigan, Sam was drafted into the army and later returned to England, de Trey remained for a time and helped to establish the School for American Craftsmen at Dartford, New Hampshire, along with Mrs Webb, founder of the World Crafts Council.

By 1945 Marianne was able to rejoin Sam in England and together they established a pottery at the Bulmer Brickyard near Sudbury in Suffolk. Here they made slipware and Marianne was able to get the proper throwing experience she needed. However, they soon required more space for their production and Bernard Leach, who had been living in 'The Cabin' at Dartington (and where he had written much of his seminal *A Potters Book*), suggested they take over the tenancy and re-establish the abandoned Shinners Bridge Pottery, which Leach started before the war. It had been initiated by Leonard and Dorothy Elmhirst, the founders of the arts community at Dartington, as part of their grand plan for the crafts on their estate. A small number of pots were initially produced, with Marianne beginning to work on a domestic slipware and tin glazed range.

While awaiting materials for a new salt kiln, Sam had converted the wood fired kiln to oil and built a small electric one for Marianne's slipware. Alas, their new life together in Devon was about to come to an abrupt end. In March 1948, Sam Haile, one of the most progressive artist-potters of his generation and who had always lived life dangerously and to the full, was killed in a car accident in Dorset. Marianne was suddenly alone, and as it turned out, pregnant with their daughter Sarah.

Nevertheless, with the help of her sisters, she resolved to carry on, and was able to develop production so that by 1950 Shinners Bridge had several employees making a domestic earthenware range for both local and national markets. A variety of slip-decorated and tin glaze plates, mugs and jugs were produced, pots which had a sense of period optimism in their shapes and decoration, reflecting the design exuberance engendered by the 1951 Festival of Britain and the new ceramic experimentation that followed the war. The new sense of creative enterprise was fuelled by such initiatives as the International Craft Conference held at Dartington in 1952, which Marianne attended and where she saw, for the first time, the consciously modernist pots of Lucie Rie (which excited her) and watched Hamada's memorable teapot-making demonstrations (*'quite awe-inspiring in the fluidity and ease with which he worked'*). Through the fifties a variety of tablewares were decorated in abstract, foliate and flower, fish and bird designs, some derived from the watercolours Marianne had made in the United States, but all reflecting the broader trends in decorative art in these years.

In 1957 disaster struck. Due to faulty wiring the pottery burnt down – literally overnight – leaving Marianne wondering whether it was worth carrying on. But this tenacious potter decided – with the crucial aid of the Dartington Trustees – to rebuild the workshop. Production soon resumed, this time in oxidised stoneware. Several variously styled ranges were produced, the most successful of which was the succinctly designed, simply decorated **Pattern I**, with its tin bearing glaze and manganese slip, that sold consistently well at the Design Centre in London. There were also abstractly painted white-glazed wares with a distinctly Mediterranean flavour, and Marianne's ability with a brush was explored in a long-running series of press-moulded individual plates, bowls and dishes with duck, plant and cockerel motifs. Shinners Bridge became important for two reasons; under Marianne's aegis, with its small team of staff, it provided a vital apprenticeship scheme (along with production potteries like Winchcombe and Crowan, St Ives and Avoncroft) for aspiring potters that was still comparatively rare. Secondly, it was making, with the able support of assistants like Frank Middlebrook and Colin Kellam (who both built new kilns), a choice of well conceived and robust tablewares that were part of the backbone of studio pottery at this time, finding outlets not only at Dartington, but at the Design Centre, Heals and the Bristol Guild.

By the sixties Marianne's individual work was being made principally for flowers, influenced as she was by the floral arrangements and demonstrations of Emily Thomas at Dartington Hall who had, Marianne wrote, *'an instinctive understanding of pots combined with great sensitivity for flowers'*. Michael Casson's *Pottery in Britain Today* (1967) illustrated de Trey's fluted and cut sided bowls, vases and dishes, some of which were almost Scandinavian in their restraint and purity. The use of rich ash and tenmoku glazes lent some of her pots an obliquely oriental quality, though Marianne was never much drawn to Bernard Leach's aesthetic. Her preference for economy at this time gave the work a distinct modernity, modern pots for modern living, and which were inexpensive to buy. If her stylistic approach was rather different to Leach's, her philosophy about making good handmade work available to the broadest market was not. It was an outlook that involved her in numerous other initiatives like the Craft Potters Association, and closer to home, the Devon Guild and the establishment of the Dartington Pottery Training Workshop in 1976.

The DPTW, based in adjacent premises at Shinners Bridge (and eventually to occupy Marianne's workshop), aimed to provide both a sound apprenticeship for would-be production potters, and a well-designed, modestly priced domestic ware. It went on to operate as a more commercial enterprise, Dartington Pottery, which finally closed in 2005.

With the eventual closure of Shinners Bridge Pottery in 1980 and de Trey's move to a much smaller studio, domestic production ceased and Marianne began to focus on her distinctive individual work, in which she was able to further investigate her graphic skills with vivid brushwork. As well as larger stoneware dishes, she has concentrated on numerous bowls and bottle shapes in delicate porcelain, animated with colourful wax resist and slips, with others in an understated fluted celadon '*for relaxation*', among the most quietly elegant pots she has made.

Looking back over Marianne de Trey's long career, what can we say about the pots? With some potters there is a consistency of style and approach throughout their life – look at David Leach or Richard Batterham for example. But Marianne is different. She has moved on in stages, in related but quite distinct phases, her pottery reflecting changing fashions and attitudes, but also her undiminished curiosity about new techniques, about very different approaches to form and glazing. The early vibrant slipware, comparable to what was being made at Winchcombe, but with a vigour of its own, already showed Marianne's abilities as a decorator and draughtswoman, one who was well-grounded in two-dimensional art before she turned to clay. It undoubtedly showed too the influence of her husband Sam Haile and his originality as a painter and a trailer of slip.

The earthenware and stoneware domestic ranges that successively underpinned the life of the pottery were notable for their stylistic diversity, from the minimally glazed stoneware (the most commercially successful), to the more exuberant items with painted and resist decoration, but all distinctly un-Leachian, distinctly un-oriental. These pots seemed just as receptive to developments in industry and modern design, both here and in Scandanavia. They were reflective of a very undogmatic and pragmatic potter who has taken many of her ideas from outside ceramics too, concerned to make pots that would enhance the modern interior as well as daily rituals.

Yet despite this variety, there is a continuity in her work as well. The graceful porcelain bowls made in more recent years – some in mixed colour clays, others incised and carved – echo the more austere forms that first emerged in the 1960s. Her other, more elaborate porcelain, embellished by intricate, often dense colour and pattern, relate back to the detailed abstract and representational motifs she has used at earlier periods. Marianne has of course been deeply concerned with overall design, but she is perhaps primarily a *linear* potter, one most distinguished by her ability to enrich and give life to surface.

The domestic intimacy and spirit of Marianne de Trey's pottery, her exploration of ceramic form and decoration, reflects over sixty years of commitment to the art of clay. Her contribution to life at Dartington, where she has been the main thread of ceramic continuity since the war, and to the well-being of the crafts in general, is testimony to her belief that the handmade should exist, not only to be useful, but to enrich and enliven our visual and tactile experience in an alienated world.

David Whiting

Marianne de Trey in her studio, c1980

I've always had to do something with my hands. When I was a child I started by learning to knit and crochet, and I made clothes for dolls from about the age of eight. We had what

The de Trey family: Anne, Yvonne, Robert, Marianne, Peter and Judy with their mother, Emma, 1918

was called a sewing maid (we were a very large family) and I learnt to sew by watching her. She made me make every stitch exactly the same and I thought there was something radically wrong if they weren't. That was my introduction to craftsmanship. My father was a businessman who would have liked to have been an architect. He was very particular about the use of tools so very early on we learnt the difference between a screwdriver and a chisel, and were taught to look after our bicycles at the age of eight or nine. There was an emphasis on *right-doing*, on treating materials and implements of whatever kind in the right sort of way. But there was danger in this. The business of sewing with tiny stitches and getting things absolutely right is a snare and a delusion as far as craftsmen are concerned because one becomes too tight and thereby diminishes the possibility of creativity, and I still find it difficult not to get caught in this trap. I think potters are lucky, luckier maybe than somebody like a furniture-maker for whom **craft** is essential – a drawer that doesn't open and shut is a disaster. For potters,

it's not so rigid. You are free to experiment and you may produce something that is wonderfully exciting but is not, if you're being really critical, terribly well made.

As part of a very conventional upbringing I was sent to a strict boarding school. The art teacher there was the only person interested in what I was going to do next. She said, '*You must go to the Royal College of Art*'. So I went to the Royal College of Art. We hear a lot nowadays about careers, but I landed up at the RCA simply because my art teacher took some interest. Arriving there, straight from school, I found myself totally in the dark without a clue as to what I was supposed to be doing. Everyone else seemed quite happy and confident. I escaped over and over again from the College into the Victoria and Albert Museum. (In those days, there was a special door through from one to the other.) So when I was supposed to be doing X, Y or Z, I was in the Museum just looking at things. I was tremendously excited by all the amazing patterns. I wasn't especially drawn to pots but to textiles, getting a diploma by the skin of my teeth at the end of the third year.

I met my husband, Sam Haile, at the Royal College. He was everything I wasn't. He had not been brought up in the same way; he thought all upper-middle class standards were crazy and was a revolutionary in practically every sense. He introduced me to serious music and all kinds of things which my background had skated over, because it was somehow dangerous ground. It was wonderful but frightening, and when I married him I thought I really was in for trouble and I was! But it was so rewarding and enlightening that I put up with the problems because of the excitement of it all, and I gradually began to understand a little more.

He was anti-war. When we married in 1938 one could feel the beginnings of danger; Hitler was powerful already. We left England just

Sam Haile, 1938

before the war started and went to America. I would, had I not married him, have stayed at home and done my duty, because I still felt that there were things I ought, or ought not, to do. In America I started to learn about pottery instead. After a difficult time for a year and a half or so, Sam held an exhibition in New York of work that had been sent over from England and as a result was asked to teach pottery at the New York State College of Ceramics at Alfred University, perhaps the biggest US college of ceramics. I was able to use the facilities, mainly learning how to make moulds and this came in useful later.

Marianne, teaching at the Centre for Disabled Servicemen, New England, USA, 1944

Sam was called up in the American army and eventually came back to England, and I rejoined him in 1945. While I was waiting for him to be demobilised he had found a brickyard with a small pottery in Suffolk, where I went and worked. That was the first time I made pots every day and learnt any sort of fluency in throwing. Then we moved Dartington, Sam had got to know David and Bernard Leach; he used to go down to St Ives when on leave from the army. In 1946 Bernard's second wife, Laurie, who had been living at Dartington in 'The Cabin' where I still live, decided to go back to St Ives to join him and the place was free. This was a tremendous opportunity because it was as hard then as it is today to find anywhere to live. The

Sam Haile at Margaret Rey's Pottery, Wimbledon, c1936

fact that I'm still there is an indication that it's been a wonderful place to live and work.

We got the Pottery back into working order. Sam built a small electric kiln, and was trying to get the right materials to build a salt kiln. At the same time he had a part-time job with the Rural Industries Bureau, which required considerable travelling. He was advising small potteries which had been working in a traditional way on how they could make pots more suitable for contemporary life – to make the pots people wanted instead of making what they had always made. Life was changing and craftspeople need to adapt. It was on one of these trips that he was involved in a fatal road accident.

I had never really considered the question of making a living from pottery, but now I was faced with it and I was going to have a child, so I really had no alternative. I had already used the electric kiln and made a few things, and I had some assistance from my two sisters who were free at that time. One of them helped me in the Pottery and the other helped me with the baby. Gradually my techniques improved and we were able to make domestic pots which were

Judy de Trey and Betty Ardill drying recycled clay, 1950s

satisfactory – they didn't leak and people liked them. If I had to do that today it would be much harder because there's so much competition. After the war people longed to have something that was different, that was handmade, that had some colour on it. During the war the only pottery available was plain white stuff; as part of the war effort potteries were not allowed to decorate any pots except for export. So our work was easy to sell and things improved. Soon I was employing three people.

For nearly ten years we continued until I began to feel that I wanted to do something slightly different. At this point there was a major setback when the Pottery burnt down. This was caused by the electric kiln, the wiring was faulty, and it happened at night, destroying the Pottery. It took me a long time to make up my mind whether to start again, but I did and it took about a year before we were operating

Marianne with Beryl Debney, daughter Sarah, the au pair and Jane Askey, 1951

again, this time making stoneware.

Potters have to make something people will buy, and that has become increasingly difficult because there is mass production of every kind. Potters today are having a difficult time compared with how it was twenty-five years ago. In the early days we made slipware, dipping the pots in a very simple way and decorating them with combing and a little slip-trailing. We also made some tin-glazed pots. With this technique, instead of a transparent glaze, an opaque glaze is used and the brush decoration is done with metallic oxides on top of the glaze.

Our production increased; we made hundreds of dishes about 5 inches across, fired face to face, ten or twelve of them on top of another. I decorated some myself, but one of the problems was to evolve decorations that other people could do. If you employ people, you have to work out a system where they are reasonably happy doing things that can be done quickly

Dinah Dunn (later married to the potter, Richard Batterham) worked with Marianne for a year, c1955

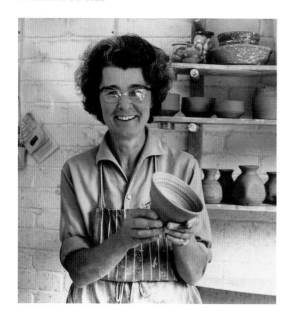

Above left: Marianne in her studio, 1971

Above right: architectural tile panel by Marianne, Shinners Bridge, c1975

Left: Marianne demonstrating throwing on the Rural Industries Bureau stand at the Exeter Agricultural Show, 1959

'The Cabin' built for Bernard Leach and designed by Bernard Leach and Rex Gardner, c1935. The extension on the right was Sam Haile's studio, built in 1946

Earthenware coffee set, black slip and tin glaze, with Sgraffito decoration, 1955

Stoneware punchbowl set in Number 1 pattern, 1960-80

Stoneware with brush stroke decoration, c1970

*Small tin glazed plates painted with floral subjects,
c1950-55*

and successfully. There were also press-moulded square dishes about 10 inches across, of which we made many hundreds. Then there was a strange period, I think as a result of the Festival of Britain in 1951, when everybody was trying to do something different and new. We evolved a technique using a semi-transparent glaze on top of a dark slip, scratching through and waxing and so on. I don't like the look of this now but we thought it was rather clever at the time. We also made a lot of lamps using wax-resist decoration. Playing around with different techniques was very valuable to me later on.

One of the influences on my work was the International Conference of Craftsmen in Pottery and Textiles, the first of its kind, held at Dartington in 1952. Craftsmen and women from Europe, Africa and Japan, most of Bernard Leach's choice, attended. It was remarkable for me chiefly for my first encounter with Bernard's Japanese colleagues, Hamada and Yanagi – Hamada with his eye-opening demonstrations and modesty, and Yanagi remarkable for the clarity of his philosophy. Lucie Rie was there also, with a s election of her work which I saw for the first time. Although Bernard was a good friend and gave me much-needed help, I had never felt inclined to make pots in the Eastern tradition, and I was impressed to see Lucie's cool acceptance of Europe and the twentieth-century, proof that something different might also be valid.

We changed from earthenware to stoneware so that customers would be happier with its hardness and durability, its sheer practicality. We made a range of black-and-white pots for about fifteen years and they were shown at the Design Centre in London a number of times. By today's standards the range was very wide: we made four different-sized cups and saucers and about four different mugs, three different plates, and about five different jugs. Black was put on as a raw glaze before it was fired, then it was waxed and dipped in the white. It was a simple technique but it had to be done just right. We

Emily Thomas and Marianne, c1975

also did a range specifically for flowers, as a result of flower-arranging classes at Dartington.

The fact that I made a series of pots specially for flower arranging deserves explanation. For many years the Trustees of Dartington Hall had a jewel, Emily Thomas, the wife of the butler and who had an instinctive understanding of pots combined with great sensitivity for flowers. She had access to Leonard Elmhirst's collection of pots and would use a Sung bowl of a little Japanese treasure for her demonstrations, and her pupils would then want something similar.

One of the things you discover as a professional potter is the complexity of the technical side – each clay is different and the glaze materials vary. One is continually testing and re-testing to avoid those disasters that beset potters without warning. Later, we got a small oil-fired kiln, and then we built a wood-fired kiln. This was when Colin Kellam was working with me. We did a lot more experimenting which I couldn't possibly have done had I not had a very good team of workers, among them Frank

Frank Middlebrook with his clay drying construction, c1960

The kiln shed, Shinners Bridge Pottery, c1970

Middlebrook, a wonderful thrower who worked with me for about eighteen years as a kind of works manager. He kept the orders organised so that we made the right numbers of everything, giving me time to do more experimental work. Colin Kellam was an extraordinarily energetic young man and a very competent thrower. He was always wanting to try something different, and he built a wood-fired kiln in the backyard which we used for ten or more years. This was where the real magic came in – it was a wonderful experience to fire a wood kiln, very demanding. The amount of air, the amount of fuel, how

For a short period, Colin and I produced tall lamps which were not handmade at the first stage. We would go over to Candy's Pipe Works, near Bovey Tracey, a factory which extruded pipes, some quite thin, some absolutely enormous. We bought what we wanted at a ridiculously cheap price as they came off the machines. They were unfired but made of rather hard clay. Colin made some very good lamps out of them, but I found the clay a bit much for the muscles in my arms and hands.

I used to have solo exhibitions when I could fit in the time and I liked to have some forms I

Colin Kellam with his Raku kiln, c1965

often you filled the firebox, all the variations were important and subtle, It was this kiln that I enjoyed more than anything else. There was a very special atmosphere in the workshop when the fire was going.

Slip-decorated earthenware lamp bases in black, grey and white, H30.5cm, 1950s

13

Production earthenware, tin glazed teaset, c1955

Red earthenware jugs, the cream slip with Sgraffito designs, c1955

Group of pre-1958 tin glazed earthenware jugs with green brush work

Impressed patterns on stoneware, H40.5cm, c1970

Wax resist pattern on a stoneware bottle, c1970

Stoneware bottle with applied relief decoration, c1970

Wood fired, handbuilt stoneware pots, c1970

Earthenware lamp base with Sgraffito decoration through white slip, H22.5cm, c1957

could concentrate on as a series, variations on a theme, which I still find is a nice approach. I do not have lots of glazes and a hundred colours, as some people do today. I find it is better to be restricted to using as few as possible and getting the most out of each.

In many ways, I don't really feel I've got to the end. It's time I stopped because I'm pretty old and I'm not quite as able as I used to be. I have to confine myself to making fairly small things; I've wrecked my thumbs, as most potters do. But I still want to go on, because there are still things I want to try. All potters go through

different stages, but in a sense we go on trying to do the same thing because we want to produce work which has a certain quality to it – that intangible, elusive something that makes it good.

I was interested in a quotation by Peter Voulkos, who was a revolutionary figure in American pottery in the sixties. He had a good training and he produced wonderful, enormous casseroles, very well made. But then he decided that this just wasn't what he wanted to do:

'Once I put a line on a plate and the thing looked good. "It was so easy, I think I'll do it again," I said, but it never happened. I tried and tried. Pretty soon the goddam thing was covered in lines.'

That puts it very well: you can't do the thing by trying, you can't do it by not trying. You have to have the experience, the technique, but that isn't really all. There is something else.

I have lived at Dartington as a tenant for forty-eight years, and the only demand on me has been to pay the rent regularly – no interference, not even a quibble about rebuilding the Pottery after I had burnt it down, only every encouragement to continue and to enjoy all that Dartington has to offer.

Potters have a crazy type of passion. They put up with very little money, hard physical work (some of it monotonous), they accept all kinds of disappointment and disasters and all because of the magical moments and the occasional sense of real achievement. The satisfaction comes through the use of every part of oneself, hand and eye, brain and intuition, and through being always in contact with natural materials and the power of earth, air, fire and water. It makes one aware also of worldwide traditions and artifacts, of their similarities and differences. It is, in fact, a voyage of discovery into the very heart of things. How lucky we are.

Marianne de Trey

The potter's hands, 1993

EARTHENWARE 1947 - 1957
SLIP DECORATED AND TIN GLAZED

Production slipware, c1950 (black and white image)

Slipware with trailed decoration, fish dish 14cm

Sgraffito decorated slipware, D27cm

Mugs with coloured slip

Tin glazed with brushed cobalt oxide and wax resist, jug 10cm

Wax resist decoration. In daily use at 'The Cabin'

Three sizes of plates, largest 24cm

Two views of a presentation bowl with Sgraffito through a black slip and tin glaze, D27cm

A SELECTION OF BRUSHWORK DECORATION IN COLOURED OXIDES ON A TIN GLAZE

D15cm

D21cm

D15cm

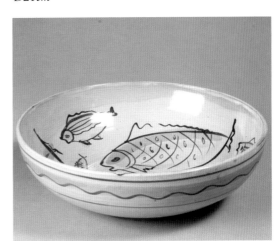

D28.5cm

D21cm

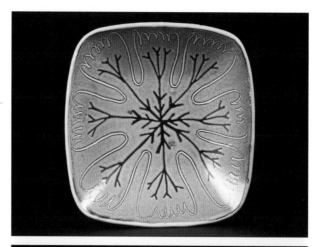

Dish 21cm

Vase 15cm

PRESS MOULDED DISHES AND THROWN SHAPES WITH BROWN MANGANESE SLIP, SGRAFFITO DECORATION AND AN OPAQUE WHITE TIN GLAZE

Black and white image

OXIDISED STONEWARE 1958 - 1983
PRODUCTION WARE - THROWN AND PRESS MOULDED SHAPES

Pattern A, wax resist with sponging and Sgraffito, large plate D17.5cm

Pattern 1, tin and manganese glazes, cream jug 8cm

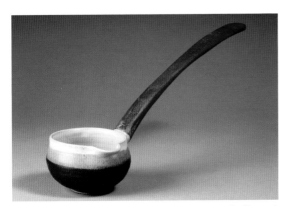

Pattern 1, ladle with original wooden handle

Pattern 5, painted decoration, bowl D22cm

Pattern 5, painted decoration, jug 9cm

D13.5cm

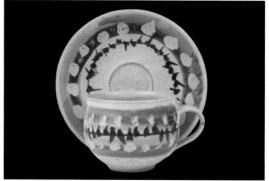

21cm

Pattern 4, Birds on a Wire

Manganese slip, D25cm

Wax resist, manganese slip, bottle 24cm

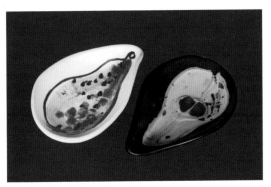

Pear dish right, cuerda secca technique, 12cm

Tin glazed brushed with coloured oxides, 16cm

Press moulded dish, brushed coloured oxides, 26cm

Brush work

Deep blue slip and Sgraffito

Trials: commercial tiles with tin glaze and Sgraffito, 15cm

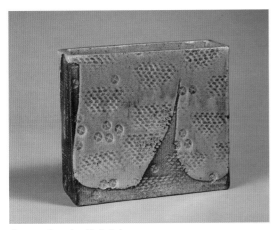

Stamped and rolled slab pot

Planter with impressed decoration, 21cm

Bonsai trays, left 27cm

Stamped and rolled decoration, 13cm

Painted with iron slip, 15cm

White slip and copper oxide, 32cm

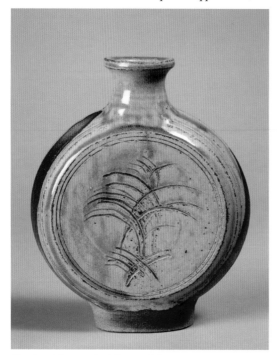

Bottle with scratched design, 21cm

26cm

Wood ash glaze, 20cm

Slab built, wood fired kiln, 24cm (C.H. Coll)

A vase of Chinese form, 16cm (C.H. Coll)

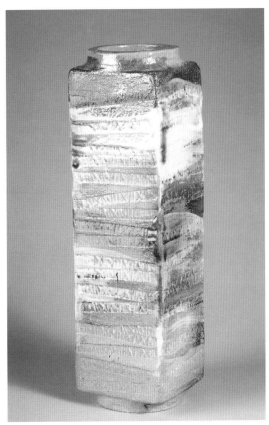

Above: brushed slip and rolled patterns, 33cm

Left: unglazed with scratched decoration, 14cm

WOOD FIRED VASES, ASH GLAZES

Stamped decoration

Stamped decoration, 17cm

Poured glaze, 17.5cm

Top: finger-wiped slip, 23cm (C.H. Coll)

Middle: wax resist and iron slip, D25cm

Bottom: wax resist and iron slip, 25cm (C.H. Coll)

TENMOKU
STONEWARE CUT-SIDED BOWLS AND VASES WITH A RICH T ENMOKU GLAZE, 1970s

21cm (C.H. Coll)

H8cm

D15cm

H7cm

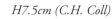

H7.5cm (C.H. Coll)

Press Moulded Stoneware Dishes
Wax resist and coloured slips (13cm) 1970s - present

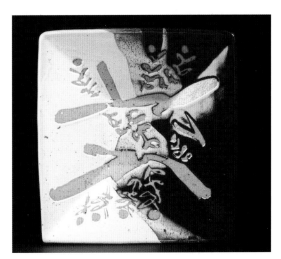

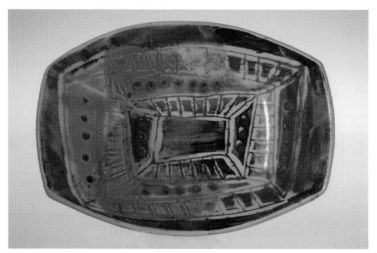

Press moulded, 37.6cm (C.H. Coll)

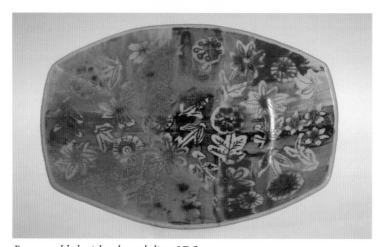

Press moulded with coloured slips, 37.5cm

37.5cm (A.C. Coll)

30cm (C.H. Coll)

(C.H. Coll)

30cm

Dartington Pottery dish, 36cm, 2006

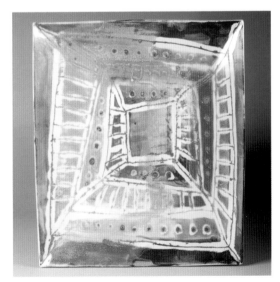

Dartington Pottery dish, 35cm, 2006

33

CELADON 1980 - PRESENT
A SERIES OF PORCELAIN BOWLS AND VASES WITH PALE CELADON GLAZES AND STAMPED AND INCISED DECORATION

Stamped decoration, 11cm

9cm

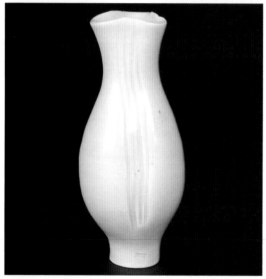

14cm

11cm

6cm

8cm

Chinese water bottle shape, 16cm

Incised decoration, 13cm

Wood ash glaze, D10cm

Wood ash glaze, D10cm

Incised leaves, D10cm

Wood ash glaze, D16cm

Fluted bowl, D16cm

D16cm

D16cm

Stamped decoration, D9cm

Stamped decoration, H17cm

Five-sided bowl shaped with a wooden tool, D11cm

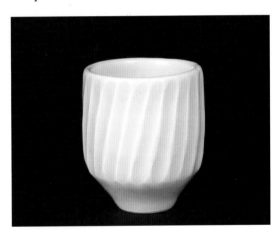

H8cm

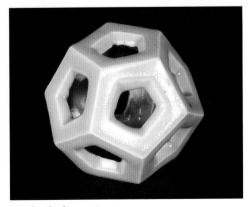

Dodecahedron, 10cm

PORCELAIN 1980 - PRESENT
REDUCTION FIRED PORCELAIN THROWN WITH COLOURED CLAYS, THROWN AND FORMING SPIRAL PATTERNS

15cm

11cm

17cm

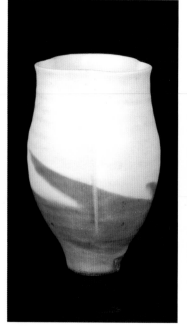

10cm

Above: blue bowl, D17cm

Left: D7.5cm

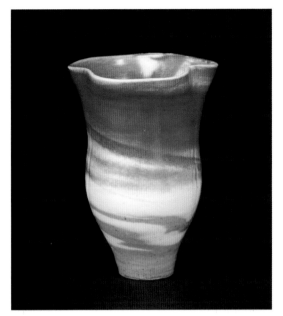

10cm

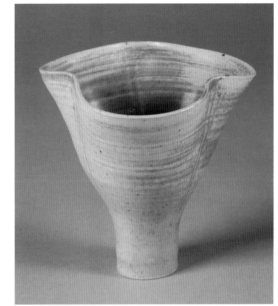

Remixed coloured clay, 10cm (C.H. Coll)

D11cm

D12cm

D17cm

**REDUCTION FIRED PORCELAIN: A RANGE OF THROWN BOTTLES, BOWLS AND VASES WITH
GEOMETRIC, LINEAR AND STYLISED FLORAL DECORATION IN COMBINATIONS OF WAX RESIST -
PAINTED WITH COLOURED SLIP, SGRAFFITO AND BRUSH WORK LUSTRES**

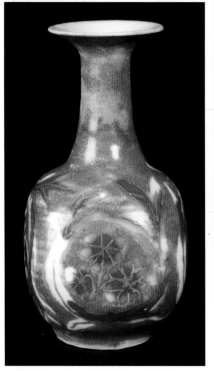

Thrown and shaped, 17cm

15cm

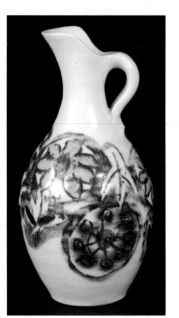

Left: 16.5cm
Middle: 10cm
Right: 13.5cm

15cm

12cm

10cm

8.5cm (C.H. Coll)

With lustre, H10.5cm (A.C. Coll)

D13.5cm (C.H. Coll)

Peacock eye decoration, 15cm

H14cm

H12cm

D16cm (C.H. Coll)

D14.5cm (C.H. Coll)

D18cm

With lustre, D8cm (A.C. Coll)

D20cm (A.C. Coll)

12cm

D16cm

D16cm

H8.5cm (C.H. Coll)

D16cm

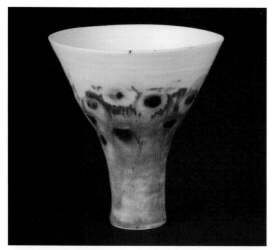

Copper spots, H10cm

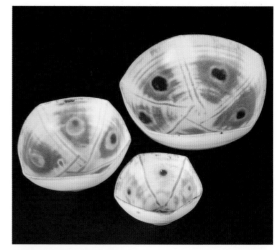

Largest bowl, D10.5cm

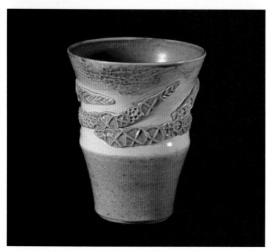

Salt glaze with applied decoration, H8cm

Copper brush work, D15.5cm (C.H. Coll)

Salt glaze with applied decoration, H8cm

Coloured clay, H5cm

Sgraffito decoration, H11cm (C.H. Coll)

Hatched scratching inlaid with copper, D9cm

D12cm (C.H. Coll)

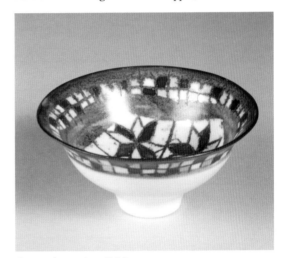

Lustre decoration, D12cm

D22cm (A.C. Coll)

D11cm

D17.5cm

With lustre, D13cm

D20cm

With lustre, D17cm

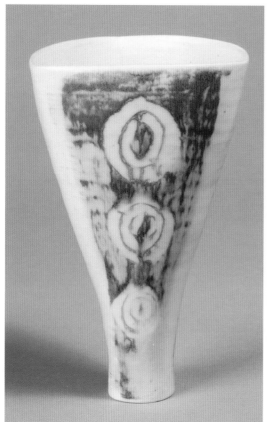

H15.5cm

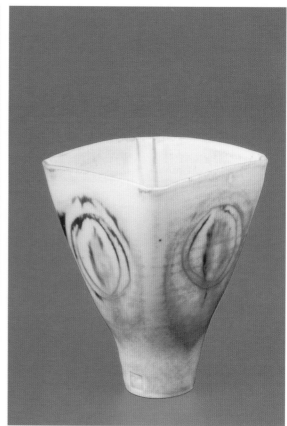

H9cm

H14cm

D19cm

Linear decoration, the matt glaze turns the copper-red slip pink, tallest bottle 27cm

MINIATURES

A GROUP OF MINIATURE PORCELAIN BOWLS AND VASES DISPLAYING A VARIETY OF TECHNIQUES AND DECORATION AS FOUND ON LARGER POTS. THE APPEAL AND CHARM OF THE MINIATURE KNOWS NO BARRIERS. SOME WERE MADE AS TRIALS.

The shell mark was used principally on production pieces, from the beginning and in different versions.

Marianne's personal marks impressed, and sometimes found with the shell mark.

The Raku kiln with John Reeve, the Canadian potter

Raku pots from Marianne and Colin Kellam were often made with students from Dartington - usually for pleasure rather than profit!

CHRONOLOGY

1913   Born in London of Swiss parents.

1932-6 Studied at the Royal College of Art in the School of Design specialising in textiles: awarded ARCA.

1937   Taught textile design at Ipswich School of Art.

1938   Married Sam Haile (1909-48), potter and painter.

1939   Travelled with Haile to Switzerland: moved with Haile to USA.

1941   Moved with Haile to New York State College of Ceramics, Alfred University, New York State: started making pottery.

1942   Moved with Haile to the College of Architecture, University of Michigan, Ann Arbor, Michigan.

1944   Helped start the School for American Craftsmen at Dartford, New Hampshire for Mrs Vanderbilt Webb, founder of the World Craft Council.

1945   Returned to England. Became a full-time potter with Haile at the Bulmer Brickyard, Sudbury, Suffolk.

1947   Moved to Shinners Bridge Pottery, Dartington and settled in 'The Cabin', both formerly occupied by Bernard Leach.

1948   Sam Haile died in a road accident. Daughter Sarah born. Started production at Shinners Bridge Pottery with help of sister, Judy de Trey.

1952   Participated in the International Conference of Craftsmen in Pottery and Textiles, Dartington Hall.

c1955 Founded the Devon Guild of Craftsmen with a small group of other craftsmen.

1957   Pottery destroyed by fire.

c1957 Became a member of the newly established Craftsmen Potters Association.

1958   Rebuilt the Pottery: changed from earthenware to oxidised stoneware production and added a small oil-fired kiln for her personal work.

1960-70 Regularly supplied the Design Centre and Heal's London.

1960   Exhibited at the Boymans-van Beuningen Museum, Rotterdam.

1964   Attended conference of the World Crafts Council in New York.

1970   Visited Greece with Michael Cardew to advise Francis Noel-Baker on setting up a pottery in Evia.

1973-5 Chaired the Devon Guild of Craftsmen.

1975   Advisor to and Board Member of Dartington Pottery Training Workshop.

1978   Attended pottery conference in Syracuse, New York State, USA.

1980   Solo exhibition at Galerie de Proen, Amsterdam.

1981   Visited China with Craftsmen Potters Association.

81/3/5 Exhibited at Kettle's Yard, Cambridge in exhibitions organised by Henry Rothschild.

1983-4 Solo exhibition 'Half a Lifetime' at Dartington and Bristol Guild.

1986   Visited Thailand with Craftsmen Potters Association.

1988   Exhibited in 'The Leach Tradition', Galerie Besson, London.

1990   Solo show at Bettles Gallery, Ringwood.

1992   Solo exhibition at Devon Guild of Craftsmen, Bovey Tracey.

2000   Awarded an Honorary Degree of Doctorate of Arts at the University of Plymouth.

2005   Participated in the International Ceramics Festival at Aberystwyth.

2006   Appointed a Commander of the British Empire (CBE). Invested by Prince Charles, March 15th.

A door handle by Rex Gardner in 'The Cabin'